Robin Hood and the Babes in the Wood

A Pantomime in Four Acts

K. O. Samuel

A SAMUEL FRENCH ACTING EDITION

SAMUELFRENCH-LONDON.CO.UK
SAMUELFRENCH.COM

Copyright © 1933 by Samuel French Ltd
All Rights Reserved

ROBIN HOOD AND THE BABES IN THE WOOD is fully protected under the copyright laws of the British Commonwealth, including Canada, the United States of America, and all other countries of the Copyright Union. All rights, including professional and amateur stage productions, recitation, lecturing, public reading, motion picture, radio broadcasting, television and the rights of translation into foreign languages are strictly reserved.

ISBN 978-0-573-06447-0

www.samuelfrench-london.co.uk

www.samuelfrench.com

FOR AMATEUR PRODUCTION ENQUIRIES

UNITED KINGDOM AND WORLD
EXCLUDING NORTH AMERICA
plays@SamuelFrench-London.co.uk
020 7255 4302/01

Each title is subject to availability from Samuel French,

depending upon country of performance.

CAUTION: Professional and amateur producers are hereby warned that *ROBIN HOOD AND THE BABES IN THE WOOD* is subject to a licensing fee. Publication of this play does not imply availability for performance. Both amateurs and professionals considering a production are strongly advised to apply to the appropriate agent before starting rehearsals, advertising, or booking a theatre. A licensing fee must be paid whether the title is presented for charity or gain and whether or not admission is charged.

The professional rights in this play are controlled by Samuel French Ltd, 52 Fitzroy Street, London, W1T 5JR.

No one shall make any changes in this title for the purpose of production. No part of this book may be reproduced, stored in a retrieval system, or transmitted in any form, by any means, now known or yet to be invented, including mechanical, electronic, photocopying, recording, videotaping, or otherwise, without the prior written permission of the publisher. No one shall upload this title, or part of this title, to any social media websites.

The right of K. O. Samuel to be identified as author of this work has been asserted by him in accordance with Section 77 of the Copyright, Designs and Patents Act 1988

CHARACTERS

ROBIN HOOD.
LITTLEJOHN.
ALLAN-A-DALE.
FRIAR TUCK.
SIR RICHARD (a Knight).
MARIAN (his Daughter).
THE KING.
THE JESTER.
THE BARON.
THE SHERIFF OF NOTTINGHAM.
THE LANDLORD.
BILLY }
BETTY } (the Babes).
THE NURSE.
COPPERNOB }
GINGERNUT } (two Villains).
THE FAIRY.
1ST ELF.
2ND ELF.
3RD ELF.
4TH ELF.
5TH ELF.

Chorus of Robin Hood's men, Villagers, Guests, Elves, etc.

SYNOPSIS OF SCENERY

ACT I
In Sherwood Forest.

ACT II
Outside " The Four Feathers " Inn.

ACT III
Scene 1.—The Haunt of the Elves.
Scene 2.—The Same.

ACT IV
The Hall of the Black Castle.

ROBIN HOOD AND THE BABES IN THE WOOD

ACT I

In Sherwood Forest.

(ROBIN HOOD'S *men are discovered grouped round the central figures of* LITTLEJOHN *and* ALLAN-A-DALE. *Some are reclining, others seated on logs. They are singing a drinking chorus as the* CURTAIN *rises.*)

LITTLEJOHN (*cup in hand*). To-day, my friends, is a great day. (*Cheers.*) To-day is our anniversary. (*More cheering.*) A year ago, who had heard of Robin Hood and his merry men ? (*Chorus :* No one !) And now—thanks to our leader and his- -er—*taking* ways—(*laughter*) we are respected and feared.

ALLAN (*springing up*). Here's to Robin Hood !

(*They all drink.*)

You may talk about your life on the ocean wave, but Sherwood Forest's good enough for me. Green's my colour. (*Drinks.*)

LITTLEJOHN (*rising and putting his arm round* ALLAN). Good old Allan. You'll never look as green as you really are. (*Slaps him hard on the back.*)

(ALLAN, *annoyed, chokes over his drink. A horn is blown off stage.*)

Here comes Robin Hood !

(*The men rise. Music for* ROBIN HOOD'S *entrance.*)

ROBIN (*coming* C., *between* ALLAN (R.) *and* LITTLEJOHN (L.)). Well, boys, what d'you know ?

LITTLEJOHN.   There's a party of merchants passing through the forest, master.   We might get a bag or two if we wait till dusk.

ROBIN (*laughing*).   Why wait till dusk ?   *I* didn't. (*He unhooks a bag of money from his belt and tosses it up.*) Feel the weight of that !

ALLAN (*catching the bag*).   I hope, sir, you came by this honestly.

(*Laughter from everybody.*)

ROBIN (*taking back the bag*).   It cost me a couple of arrows.   The old gentleman trembled so much that his money-bags simply—dropped off.

LITTLEJOHN.   And you—er—picked them up.

ROBIN.   Of course.

ALLAN.   But there's only one bag here, master.

ROBIN.   Doesn't do to bleed 'em too much.   I take one egg, and leave two in the nest.

LITTLEJOHN (*anxiously*).   I hope you didn't use *new* arrows.

ROBIN.   Why not ?

LITTLEJOHN.   Well, master, you know about our shortage of arrows just now.   Surely a couple of re-paints would have been good enough in this case.

ROBIN.   Good Littlejohn, I stand corrected.   I had forgotten I had made you Master of Munitions.

LITTLEJOHN.   We must economize in these times, master.   It makes me think of that song that used to annoy me so much.

ROBIN.   What song ?

LITTLEJOHN (*singing*).   " I shot an arrow into the air.   It fell to earth I know not where."   Such a waste ! (*Shakes his head sadly.*)

ROBIN (*laughing*).   Send for Friar Tuck and let me confess my sin.

ALLAN (*looking off* R.).   No need to send, master, for here comes the worthy friar.

(FRIAR TUCK, *who is the droll rather than the jovial type, enters* R., *pulling behind him a toy dog on wheels.   A*

*tin for pennies hangs from the dog's neck, with a notice,
" Robin Hood's Hospital.   1,000 pounds wanted."   A
few bars of music for the* FRIAR'S *entrance.)*

FRIAR (*coming* C. *to* ROBIN).   Robin, my boy, I've had
a bad round to-day.   (*He unhooks the tin from the dog's
neck and counts the contents.*)

(ALLAN *comes down* R.)

Fourpence in cash, three trouser-buttons and a couple
of golf tees.
    ROBIN (*laughing*).   That won't do the Hospital much
good.
    FRIAR (*dismally*).   And apart from the Hospital—
what's the good of trouser-buttons to *me* !   (*Holds out
his gown.*)   People I stopped on the road said they had
never heard of Robin Hood's hospital.   They said they'd
be most happy to give to a *good* hospital like (*mention
local hospital*)—but they wouldn't give to mine !
    ROBIN.   You're no good, friar.   People will always
give money if you talk to them nicely—like I do.   (*Holds
up the money-bag.*)

(FRIAR TUCK *grunts in disgust, leads his dog up* L. *and
proceeds to brush and comb it.*)

(*Looking at the bag wistfully.*)   I think perhaps we'd
better put this in the old oak chest.

(*Murmurs of disappointment from the men.*)

On second thoughts, perhaps we'll share it out amongst
the rest.   (*Tosses bag to* ALLAN.)   Here, Allan, I rely
on you to see that each of our merry men gets a fair
share.

(*The men cheer, form up and march off, singing the chorus
of their opening number,* ALLAN *with the money-bag
leading the way.   They exit* R.)

(*Seated on log down* R.).   Well, Friar, have you got any
fatherly advice for me to-day ?

(FRIAR TUCK *picks up his dog and carrying it tucked*

*under his arm, comes downstage and sits on log c.,
putting the dog down.)*

FRIAR. Yes, my boy, I have. The same as usual.
Give up robbery and violence. It will get you into
trouble with the King before long.

ROBIN. You know, Friar, it's all very well for you
to go about singing " A jovial monk am I " and all
that, but if we *all* did that sort of thing we should soon
starve.

FRIAR. Have it your own way, only don't blame me
if you finish up on the gallows.

ROBIN. *Aren't* you bright and cheery this morning !
Let's change the subject, shall we ? (*Thinks a moment
and then slaps his knee.*) I've got an idea !

FRIAR. More robbery ?

ROBIN. Let's open a Road-House for Weary Trav-
ellers. "Robin Hood's Road-House." How's that ?

FRIAR (*sneering*). " Good Pull-up for Archers," eh ?

ROBIN (*rising*). And you, Friar Tuck, can be the
manager.

FRIAR (*disgustedly*). In that case you'd better call it
" The Tuck Shop."

LITTLEJOHN (*who has been upstage* L., *looking off*).
Master, a Knight is approaching.

FRIAR. *Night* is approaching ! (*Looks at his wrist.*)
But it's only just noon !

LITTLEJOHN (*coming down*). I said KNIGHT ! KER-
NIGHT. K-N-I-G-H-T ! (*Spells the word.*)

ROBIN. A knight ! This is lucky.

LITTLEJOHN (*upstage again, looking off*). And a fair
lady with him.

ROBIN. Better still ! You'd better make yourself
scarce, Friar. She's sure not to like your face.

(FRIAR TUCK *glares at him, and goes off* R., *pulling his
dog after him.*)

LITTLEJOHN. He has no horse, master, which is
strange, and the lady is walking, too.

ROBIN (*down* R.). What is she like ?

LITTLEJOHN. Very bee-utiful, master!

(Robin *becomes concerned about his appearance, brushes himself down, sets his cap at a rakish angle and stands waiting.* Littlejohn *has crossed* R. *and stands above* Robin.)

(Sir Richard *enters* L., *followed by* Marian.)

Sir Richard.   Let us rest here awhile, daughter, and save our strength.

(Sir Richard *sees* Robin Hood *and stops.   They regard each other.*)

(*After a pause.*)   Who are you, stranger, who stares so rudely ?

Robin.   Your pardon, Sir Knight, I was only admiring the lady.

Sir Richard.   This is no time nor place for compliments.   We are weary and in trouble.

Robin.   Then you have come to the right man.

Sir Richard.   You talk as if you owned the forest.

Robin.   I do—in a way.

Sir Richard (*staring at him*).   Humph !   (*Pointing to log* C.).   May I sit on this log ?

Robin.   There's no charge.

(Sir Richard *sits on log* C., Marian *on his* L.)

Sir Richard.   You're a cool fellow.

Robin.   I need to be.   I live by my wits.   You may have heard of me.

Sir Richard.   I don't suppose so.   I've been on the Crusades and I've lost touch with local gossip.   Who are you, anyway ?

Robin.   I am Robin Hood.

Marian (*startled*).   What !   Robin Hood, the outlaw ?

Robin (*smiling at her*).   The very same.   But I'm quite harmless.   Don't be alarmed.

Sir Richard.   I'm not alarmed.   Knights are never alarmed.

Robin.   Where is your horse ?

MARIAN. Father has had to sell his horse. We are in great trouble, sir.

SIR RICHARD. Alas, my poor horse! I bought it new. It had only done five hundred miles! But I needed the money. I'm trying to raise money, young fellow, to buy back my castle which is held in pledge by the Sheriff of Nottingham.

ROBIN. We might do a deal. I have money.

SIR RICHARD. Sir Richard does not bargain with outlaws.

ROBIN. Not if you accept their hospitality? After all, that *is my* log you're sitting on.

MARIAN. If you can offer us food and drink, sir, we shall be most grateful. We have tramped many weary miles.

ROBIN. I can offer you both. Sir Richard, what will you drink?

SIR RICHARD (*trying not to appear too eager*). Well— er, I never take anything strong. Have you any home-made lemonade? (*Rises.*)

ROBIN. Littlejohn, take Sir Richard to the canteen. I will look after the lady.

(LITTLEJOHN *leads the way off* R.)

SIR RICHARD (*following him, and mopping his brow*). *With* a piece of ice in it—if you have such a thing——

(*Exit* LITTLEJOHN *and* SIR RICHARD, R.)

ROBIN. You are very beautiful!

MARIAN. And you, sir, are not a bit—— (*She hesitates.*)

ROBIN. Not a bit beautiful?

MARIAN. Not a bit like an outlaw, I was going to say. I thought the famous Robin Hood was very bold and bad.

ROBIN (*going to her*). Instead of tender and loving— like this. (*He puts his arm round her.*)

MARIAN. I call *that* being bold!

ROBIN. And bad?

MARIAN. Not—so bad. (*Smiles.*)

(ROBIN *gives her a kiss.*)

Sir !

ROBIN.   It's the forest air, you know.   Always makes me feel like that.

MARIAN (*pushing him away*).   Then I should try a little town life, if I were you.   Perhaps the air at (*local name*) would suit you better.   Father said I was not to flirt with young men in the forest.

ROBIN.   Quite right.   I'll see that you don't.

MARIAN.   *You* will ?

ROBIN.   In Sherwood Forest my word is law.

MARIAN.   I don't know why men always want to kiss girls they hardly know.

ROBIN.   I'm different.   I seem to have known *you* for years.   You are the vision of my dreams.

(*Duet for* MARIAN *and* ROBIN HOOD.)

Listen, little one.   (*He takes her down* L.)   Your father wants money.   How much ?

MARIAN.   Five hundred pounds, to buy back his lands.

ROBIN.   I will see what can be done.

MARIAN.   Oh, Robin Hood, how can I thank you !

ROBIN.   This way.   (*Kisses her.*)

(SIR RICHARD *re-enters from* R. *and sees the embrace.*)

SIR RICHARD (*loudly*).   Ha !   You can't do that, young man !

ROBIN.   Can't I ?   I've just done it !

(SIR RICHARD *approaches him threateningly.*   MARIAN *crosses between them.*)

MARIAN.   Wait, father.   Robin Hood has offered to help us with money.

SIR RICHARD.   Why didn't he say so before ?   Well, what are your terms ?

ROBIN.   You want the money—I want the girl.

SIR RICHARD.   My daughter is not for sale.

ROBIN.   Then I will win her, and what is more, you

shall have your loan without security. I can afford to be generous. I have money in the bank. Ho, there! Littlejohn!

(LITTLEJOHN *appears* R.)

Bring in the bank!

(*Exit* LITTLEJOHN.)

SIR RICHARD. You're a remarkable young man, if I may say so.

ROBIN. I am—and you may!

(*A large chest is carried on* R. *by* LITTLEJOHN *and* ALLAN-A-DALE, *escorted by some of the men. Characteristic music can be used here to make the entrance more effective. The chest bears a large notice: "Robin Hood's Bank. Hours: 9 to 4. Open all the year round," etc.*)

(*Handing key.*) Open the bank. (*He moves* R.)

(*The chest is placed* C. *The men form up behind.* LITTLE-JOHN *and* ALLAN *are at the chest.* ROBIN HOOD *down* R. SIR RICHARD *and* MARIAN L. LITTLEJOHN *and* ALLAN *unlock the chest and pull at the lid, which sticks and then opens suddenly so that they fall backwards.*)

There's an overdraft somewhere!

LITTLEJOHN } (*recovering themselves*). The bank is
ALLAN   } open, sir.

ROBIN. Sir Richard will draw out the sum of five hundred pounds.

ALLAN. Will you have it in nold or gotes, sir?

SIR RICHARD. Goats? I don't want any goats.

LITTLEJOHN. He means gold or notes, sir.

SIR RICHARD. I will take it in gold.

(*Scales are produced and the money-bags are weighed.* ALLAN *and* LITTLEJOHN *can introduce comic business here, such as piling the bags on the scales and forgetting to put the weights on.*)

ALLAN (*holding up bags on a tray*).   Will you take them with you, sir, or shall we send them ?

(SIR RICHARD *takes the tray of bags.*)

MARIAN (*crossing* R.).   Robin Hood, you are indeed a friend in need.   (*Clasps her hands together.*)   Ah, this is too much !

ALLAN
LITTLEJOHN } (*surprised*).   Too much ?

(*They begin to put back some of the bags,* SIR RICHARD *trying to stop them.*)

MARIAN.   Too much generosity !   It is overwhelming.

SIR RICHARD.   You shall be repaid, sir, I promise you, within a year from to-day.

(*The bags are put into a large string-bag and given to* SIR RICHARD.)

ROBIN.   I grant this loan on one condition.   You shall repay me within a year and the money must be returned by the fair hand of your daughter.

SIR RICHARD.   It shall be done.   I am a Knight, and knights always keep their word.

ROBIN.   You may keep your word, Sir Richard, but you may lose your daughter.

MARIAN (*kneeling and kissing his hand*).   We accept the terms.

ROBIN.   Then we shall meet again.   Till then, as it is not right that a knight and a lady should travel alone, you shall have an escort of good Lincoln Green. Littlejohn !

(LITTLEJOHN *steps forward.*)

You can be trusted.   You shall see that they have food and drink, accompany them on their journey and take care that no harm befalls them.

(LITTLEJOHN *takes the bag of money, slings it over his shoulder and prepares to lead the way.* SIR RICHARD *watches the money anxiously.*)

MARIAN (*holding out her hand to* ROBIN HOOD *as she prepares to go*). I will spread the news that Robin Hood is a good fellow.

(ROBIN *kisses her hand. She goes off* R., *followed by* SIR RICHARD *and* LITTLEJOHN.)

ROBIN (C.). God-speed!

(SIR RICHARD *turns to acknowledge the salute, and catches sight of* LITTLEJOHN, *who is carrying the money.*)

SIR RICHARD. I think I'd better carry that myself.

(*He takes the bag from* LITTLEJOHN *and goes off, followed by* LITTLEJOHN.)

(*A song should be introduced here for* ROBIN HOOD, *supported by his men.*)

CURTAIN.

ACT II

Outside " The Four Feathers." A village Inn.

*(There are benches and tables outside the inn, and the
entrance to the inn is through a door back C.*

*Villagers are discovered in a country dance, after
which the* LANDLORD *enters from back C., followed by
the* BARON, *carrying a roll of parchment. Villagers
give way and form up each side of the stage.)*

BARON. Fetch me a table, Landlord, and writing
materials. I have important business.

LANDLORD. Yes, Baron.

*(He claps his hands and two men bring one of the tables
down* R.C.)

I—er—I hope the Baron slept well.

BARON. I never slept at all.

LANDLORD. Nothing wrong with the bed. I hope,
Baron ?

BARON. Everything was wrong with the bed. To
begin with, your servant put in a frying-pan instead of
a warming-pan.

LANDLORD. That's the new maid, sir. She hasn't
got used to the work yet. I'll scold her. (*He runs
upstage.*)

BARON. Landlord !

*(*LANDLORD *runs back to* BARON, *who is seated at the
table.)*

If it occurs again, there'll be a dent in that frying-pan
and a lump on your head.

LANDLORD (*rubbing his head*). I understand, Baron.
(*Runs upstage.*)

BARON. And—Landlord !

*(*LANDLORD *runs back again.)*

Send all this—this scum away. (*He waves his hand at the villagers.*)

(LANDLORD *obediently shoos off the villagers, who fade away* R. *and* L., *grumbling, one or two making threatening gestures at the* BARON *when his back is turned.*)

Landlord !

(LANDLORD *runs to him again.*)

If the Sheriff of Nottingham calls—show him in.
LANDLORD. You mean—show him *out*, Baron.
BARON. Nothing of the kind !
LANDLORD. But, Baron, this is " out " (*waving his hand at the table*)—that (*waving his hand at the inn door*) is " in."

(BARON, *annoyed, aims the roll of parchment at* LAND-LORD, *who ducks and runs upstage, colliding at the door with the* NURSE *who is coming out. They dodge each other for some time.*)

NURSE. Now, which way *are* you going ? Make up your mind !

(LANDLORD *disappears through door and* NURSE *comes down* C., *straightening her apron and cap.*)

Some mothers have some clumsy children. (*Sees* BARON.) And some children have some stingy uncles —if I may say so—without losing my job.
BARON. What's the matter now ?
NURSE. If I've told you once, I've told you fifty times that the two babes must have new clothes.
BARON (*thumping the table*). And I tell you once for all that I've no money to waste on baby-clothes.
NURSE. Well, don't shout. I'm not deaf. It's time something was done.
BARON. I have made my plans about the babes. It's time they were—put away.
NURSE (*horrified*). Put away !
BARON. Put away—to school. (*He smiles at his joke.*)

Nurse. They're not old enough.

Baron. They're old enough for the school *I* shall send them to. (*He faces front, looking sinister.*)

(*The* Babes *are heard laughing and chattering off stage.*)

Nurse. Here they come, the pretty dears!

(*The* Babes *enter from door back o.,* Billy *with hoop and stick, and* Betty *carrying a book.*)

Betty (*running to* Nurse *l.o.*). Hallo, Nursie!

Billy (*going to* Baron). Good morning, Uncle.

(Baron *grunts.* Billy *picks up the roll of parchment.*)

What's this, uncle ?

Baron (*snatching it from him*). Put that down. Run away and play.

Billy. But we've been playing. We're tired of playing.

Nurse. Come and talk to Nurse. You mustn't worry Uncle when he's busy.

(Billy *crosses* l., *grumbling.* Nurse *fetches a bench down* l.o., *and sits between the* Babes, Billy *on her* r. Baron *leans on the table, his head between his hands.*)

Billy (*after looking at the* Baron). Nurse, doesn't Uncle feel well ?

Nurse. Sh! Uncle's thinking.

Billy. What's he thinking about ?

Nurse. I don't know. Don't ask so many questions.

(Baron *unrolls the parchment and starts to read.*)

(*To* Betty.) Now open your book and we'll have a lesson, and then you can show Uncle what clever children you are. (Nurse *takes the book.*) What does " A " stand for ?

Billy. April Fool!

Betty (*laughing and clapping her hands*). Nursie, you're an April Fool.

(*While* Nurse *is scolding* Betty, Billy *takes out a blow-pipe and blows a pea on to the* Baron's *head.* Baron *starts, looks round behind him, scratches his head, puzzled, and then resumes his reading.*)

Nurse. " A " stands for Apple.

Betty. But it *does* stand for April Fool, doesn't it, Nurse ?

Nurse. No ! Not at this time of the year. " A " stands for Apple.

Billy. Why does it stand for Apple, Nurse ?

Nurse. Don't ask silly questions. What does " B " stand for ?

Betty. Now *you're* asking silly questions.

(Nurse *scolds* Betty *again and* Billy *blows another pea on to the* Baron's *head. Business as before.*)

(*Catching sight of the blow-pipe.*) " B " stands for Blow-pipe !

Nurse. There's no such thing.

Betty. Yes, there is. Billy's got one.

Billy. Sneak !

Nurse. What have you got there, Billy ?

Baron (*rising to his feet, with a roar*). Ah ! So it was *you*, was it ? Now *I'm* going to teach you a lesson. (*Takes off his belt.*) " B " stands for BELT ! and I'm going to give you a good belting.

(Baron *advances on* Billy, *who runs round* Nurse, *followed by* Betty. *They circle round* Nurse, *the* Baron *chasing the* Babes. *Quick music here.*)

Nurse. What d'you think *I* am—the mulberry-bush ?

(*The* Babes *break away and crawl under the table. The* Baron *thumps the table with his belt.*)

Baron. Come out of your holes, you little foxes !

(*He waits at one end of the table while the* Babes *crawl out on the other side and make for the exit* R. *on their hands and knees.* Baron *sees them and gives a yell.*)

They're off !

(*He rushes out after them, followed by* NURSE. *The stage is left empty. Music for entrance of the two* VILLAINS. *They enter from* L. *and sing a characteristic duet, introducing themselves.*)

COPPERNOB (*looking round him*). We don't seem to be expected, do we ?

GINGERNUT. This is the rondivoo.

COPPERNOB. The—the what ?

GINGERNUT. The rondivoo.

COPPERNOB. What's that ?

GINGERNUT. Don't you know what a rondivoo is ? Where's yer French ?

COPPERNOB. What's it mean ?

GINGERNUT. It's—er—it's French, you see. Voo means " you " and rondi means " meet me."

COPPERNOB. I see. I've got to meet you.

GINGERNUT (*disgusted with him*). No, no ! *We've* got to meet the Baron. Let's have another look at the letter. (*Takes out letter and reads.*) " To Messrs. Coppernob and Gingernut, Limited "—that's you and me.

COPPERNOB. Why does he say " Limited " ?

GINGERNUT. That's Latin and it means there are only two of us, you see. You—Coppernob, and me— Gingernut. Aren't you dull to-day. (*Resumes reading.*) " Dear Sirs "—isn't that nice of him—" If you will meet me outside ' The Four Feathers ' at noon to-morrow, you will 'ear something to your advantage." Now then—(*looks round*)—there's " The Four Feathers."

COPPERNOB (*counting*). One, two, three, four—yes, that's right.

GINGERNUT. But where's the Baron ?

(BARON *appears at door back* C.)

BARON. Ha !

(*The* VILLAINS *jump with fright.*)

So you're here, are you ?

COPPERNOB. Yes, sir—and this is the paravoo.

GINGERNUT (*nudging him*). RONDIVOO.

(*BARON glances round him anxiously and then creeps down to table, beckoning the* VILLAINS, *who creep up one on each side of him.*)

BARON (*dramatically*). Listen !
COPPERNOB (*turning away, hand to ear*). I can't hear anything.
BARON (*pulling him back, impatiently*). Listen—to me ! You know the babes ?
COPPERNOB. A little boy ?
GINGERNUT. —and a little girl ?

(*They nod assent.*)

BARON. You've seen them playing in the wood ?
COPPERNOB
GINGERNUT } (*together*). We have.
BARON. To-morrow, they will play in the wood—for the last time. (*He pauses and gives them a meaning look.*) You understand ?
COPPERNOB
GINGERNUT } (*together*). We understand.
BARON. They must not be seen or heard of again. You can do the job in your own way. How much do you want ?
GINGERNUT. We can give you an estimate, sir.
BARON. Hurry up, there's no time to be lost.

(*The* VILLAINS *draw aside and consult, while the* BARON *gets his money ready.*)

GINGERNUT (*returning*). Fifty pounds.
BARON. I'll give you twenty pounds each. Do the job well, and perhaps we'll split the difference.
GINGERNUT. Nothing less than fifty pounds—or we'll do the splitting. (*Winks at* COPPERNOB.)
BARON (*quickly*). Here's your fifty pounds. Take it and be off.

(*He hands out a bag of money.* GINGERNUT *takes it and the two* VILLAINS *bow themselves out backwards,* L.)

GINGERNUT. 'Oping to receive further favours——

COPPERNOB. We remain——
GINGERNUT. Yours affectionately——
COPPERNOB. Coppernob——
GINGERNUT. And Gingernut——
COPPERNOB. Limited !

(Exeunt L.)

BARON (facing front). It would cost me more than fifty pounds to keep the brats alive. I've not done so badly !

(A trumpet is blown off stage.)

Here comes the Sheriff. Now to my business.

(BARON seats himself at the table again. The SHERIFF enters R., preceded by a man in the King's livery who announces: "The Sheriff of Nottingham." The SHERIFF wears on his tunic, in large type, the letters "O.H.M.S." He comes down L. of table.)

Good morning, Sheriff. We'll waste no time. I have the document ready assigning to me the castle and lands of the late Sir Richard, for the sum of five hundred pounds.

SHERIFF. That is a poor sum for such a property, Baron. (Takes the parchment and reads:) "This desirable fortification, standing in its own grounds, containing all the latest improvements for keeping out robbers and gangsters. Its wide moat and modern drawbridge, which a child can work, are proof against all gate-crashers. Its torture-chambers are unrivalled, containing the latest devices for pulling out the——"

BARON. All right, Sheriff, we won't go into details.

SHERIFF. It is worth a thousand pounds, Baron.

BARON. It's worth what you can get, and nothing more. Sign the paper.

SHERIFF (facing front). I am sorely tempted to sell. (To BARON.) But we must be careful. The castle is not mine to sell until midnight to-night. Until then, Sir Richard has the right to buy it back—if he is alive and can raise the money.

BARON. Bah! Sir Richard is dead. He went to the Crusades. They never come back! Quick, sign the paper. I must have the castle.

SHERIFF (*making up his mind*). And I must have the gold! (*He takes a bag of money from the* BARON.) My need is sore! (*He is about to sign the parchment.*)

(LANDLORD *runs on from* L.)

LANDLORD. My lord, here is a traveller to see you.

(SHERIFF *and* BARON *exchange looks.*)

SHERIFF. A traveller?

(*They look round as* SIR RICHARD *strides on* L., *followed by* LITTLEJOHN, *hiding his green tunic under a cloak.* LANDLORD *retires back* C.)

SIR RICHARD (*coming* C. *to* SHERIFF). You are the Sheriff of Nottingham.

SHERIFF. I don't know you.

SIR RICHARD (*going closer to him*). Look again.

SHERIFF (*peering at his face and giving a start of surprise*). Sir Richard! We—we thought you were dead!

SIR RICHARD. I am a knight and a man of honour. Before I die—I pay my debts.

(*He signs to* LITTLEJOHN, *on his* L., *who produces a bag of money.* SIR RICHARD *takes it and throws it on the table.*)

Now we are quits! Give me back the lands I pledged to you.

BARON (*starting up and pointing quickly at* LITTLEJOHN). Arrest that man!

SHERIFF. What's this?

(BARON *crosses to* LITTLEJOHN *and with a quick movement, tears open his cloak.*)

BARON. See! The Lincoln green! Here's one of Robin Hood's men. So, Sir Knight—you are in League with the outlaw.

(LITTLEJOHN *makes a dash for the exit* L.)

Stop thief !

(BARON *runs after* LITTLEJOHN, *who throws his cloak over
the* BARON'S *head and escapes* L.   LANDLORD *runs off*
R. *to fetch help.   The* BARON *is brought down* C. *by the*
SHERIFF'S *attendant.   Comic business here, while the*
BARON *tries to get his head out of the cloak.   When he
is free, he shouts at* SIR RICHARD.)

You've come too late !
SHERIFF.   The knight has paid his debt in time,
Baron.   The lands must be restored to him.

(SHERIFF *picks up the bag of money.*)

BARON.   Touch not the gold !   It is tainted !   A
curse will fall upon you.
SHERIFF (*between* BARON *and* SIR RICHARD, *who is
down* L.).   You must fight it out between you.   The
Sheriff does not enter into private quarrels.   In the
meantime—(*he holds up the two bags*)—I hold the gold.

(SHERIFF *winks at* SIR RICHARD, *and exits hurriedly up*
L., *followed by his attendant.*)

BARON.   Traitor !   Let me get at him !

(BARON *runs towards exit* L., *but* SIR RICHARD *is too
quick for him, gets there first and bars the way with his
sword.*)

SIR RICHARD.   Over my dead body !
BARON (*drawing back a step and blustering*).   B-but
you're not *dead* yet.   I thought you *were* dead.   (*Queru-
lously.*)   You've no right to come back alive and spoil
my plans.
SIR RICHARD.   I am an old soldier, and old soldiers
never die —they only fade away——

(*He fades away* L.)

(BARON *staggers to* C., *hands to head, clenching his fists
and raving.   The* LANDLORD *returns* R., *at the head
of the villagers, who form up in an oblique line* R.)

LANDLORD. What's the matter, Baron ? Have you got the toothache ?

BARON (*shaking his fists in the air*). Toothache ! (*He turns to the crowd.*) Good people, listen. Is it right that loyal citizens should be robbed and defrauded ?

VILLAGERS (*shouting*). No !

BARON. What is the cause of the unrest in the countryside ?

A VOICE. You are !

(BARON *glares round.*)

LANDLORD (*to crowd*). Sh !

BARON. Robin Hood is at the root of all the trouble. He has a finger in every pie. Is that right ?

VILLAGERS. No !

BARON. Shall he be allowed to roam the forest unmolested ?

VILLAGERS. No !

BARON (*getting worked up*). Will you go out and fight him ?

VILLAGERS (*monotonously*). No !

BARON (*roaring*). What ?

LANDLORD (*dictating nervously to crowd*). You ought to have said " Yes " that time.

(*There is a commotion at the back of the crowd and the two* VILLAINS *push forward.*)

GINGERNUT. What's the trouble ? Somebody fainted ?

BARON. Ah ! Just the men I'm looking for. You will go into the forest, capture Robin Hood and bring him to me.

COPPERNOB (*weakly*). What, both of us ?

BARON. Yes—unless you can do it single-handed.

(*The* VILLAINS *exchange looks of dismay and then fall back in a dead faint into the arms of the crowd.*)

LANDLORD. Somebody *has* fainted !

(*The* VILLAINS *are carried out by the villagers as the* BARON *comes down* O. *in a rage.*)

BARON. They're *all* against me! But I'll be revenged! I'll be revenged on Robin Hood and his merry men!

CURTAIN.

ACT III

Scene 1.—*Haunt of the Elves.*

(*There is a grass bank upstage, with room to pass behind.*)

(*The* Curtain *rises on a dance of the forest elves, after which they sit in a half-circle and discuss things in general.*)

1st Elf. I don't think we'll do any more dancing. It's too hot.

2nd Elf. There doesn't seem to be anything else to do, though, does there ?

1st Elf. Except sit about on tree-stumps and look interesting. I don't see that we're much use, anyway.

3rd Elf (*jumping up and looking inspired*). *We* are the spirits of the forest.

1st Elf (*laughing derisively*). *Evil* spirits, I suppose. (*Rudely.*) *You* look pretty evil at the moment.

3rd Elf (*ignoring* 1st Elf). The mortals could not do without us, and even if we did not exist they would have to invent us.

1st Elf. That's been said before. Besides—you don't really believe in all that stuff, do you ? Look at those two idiots (*points to two elves who are having a quarrel and punching each other*), I should have thought *anybody* could do without *them.*

(*The two elves are scolded by their neighbours in dumbshow and smacked, whereupon they both begin to cry.*)

3rd Elf. They're not real elves or they wouldn't cry like that. They should be asked to resign.

4th Elf. I say ! I *must* tell you ! I saw a fairy the other day.

2nd Elf. Where !

4TH ELF. Dancing about on one of those silly toad-stools, you know.

2ND ELF. Did you speak to her ?

4TH ELF. I was going to, but when she caught sight of me staring at her, she ran away.

1ST ELF. I'm not surprised.

4TH ELF. There's no need to be rude.

5TH ELF. *I've* never seen a fairy. What was she like ?

4TH ELF. Very pretty, of course. They always are, you know. She had a very short skirt on which stuck out stiffly all the way round, and she was waving a stick with a star on the end and turning round on her toes—like this !

(4TH ELF rises, tries a pirouette and falls over. General laughter from the rest.)

(*Annoyed.*) None of *you* could do it, anyway.

1ST ELF. *We're* not silly enough to try.

(4TH ELF retires upstage and sulks.)

2ND ELF. Oo I say, look ! Here comes your fairy !

(*The FAIRY enters from L. She wears a ballet skirt and carries a wand. The ELVES rise and divide as she comes C.*)

ELVES. Good morning, fairy.

FAIRY. Good morning, elves—won't you seat yours-ELVES ?

(ELVES *all laugh at the pun. The FAIRY stares at them with a puzzled expression.*)

Have I said anything wrong ?

1ST ELF. You've just made a dreadful pun, but as you haven't got a sense of humour, you can't see it.

2ND ELF. Do you know you're trespassing ?

3RD ELF. Why do you stand on one leg, when you've got two ?

4TH ELF. Where do you go when it's raining ?

5TH ELF (*pointing to wand*). What's that stick for ?

(*These questions are fired at her quickly, one after the
    other, bewildering her.*)

FAIRY. Dear me ! What a lot of questions. I can't
answer them all at once. Perhaps you had better write
them down and——

1ST ELF. I know—" questions *after* the meeting."
What we really want to know is—what are you doing
here ?

FAIRY. I've come to teach you to dance.

3RD ELF. We already dance very well, thank you.

FAIRY. No—you only hop about in a very ugly way.
Now I will show you some graceful steps.

(*The FAIRY does a Pas Seul, after which she is applauded
    by the ELVES and takes her bow. She then pauses, hand
    to ear, runs up R., looks offstage and runs back C.,
    registering fright.*)

Fly, all of you ! Danger is near. Hide yourselves !

(*Exits up L. The ELVES scatter and disappear through
    lower exits R. and L. Music of the VILLAINS' " theme."
    The VILLAINS enter from up R. They are heavily
    armed, with swords and daggers and archery equipment.
    They creep on cautiously and look about them.*)

GINGERNUT (*beckoning to COPPERNOB and bringing him
C.*). Now, Coppernob, we look harmless enough, don't
we ?

COPPERNOB. Yes, if *you* say so.

GINGERNUT. As soon as we see the babes, we must
try a little peaceful persuasion, see ?

COPPERNOB. Hadn't we better disarm, first ?

GINGERNUT. No, no. The more arms the better.
If you want peace, you must prepare for war, mustn't
you ?

COPPERNOB. Yes, if *you* say so.

GINGERNUT. Don't keep saying " if *you* say so "—
everybody says so, don't they ?

COPPERNOB (*monotonously*). Yes, if *you* say so.

(GINGERNUT *pushes him away in disgust.* COPPERNOB *puts an arrow to his bow and is about to shoot it at the audience.* GINGERNUT *pulls him back just in time.*)

GINGERNUT.   What are you doing ?
COPPERNOB.   Preparing for war.

(GINGERNUT *takes his bow away from him.*)

GINGERNUT.   You'll have us locked up as disturbers of the peace, that's what you'll do.   Now, as soon as the babes come along you must engage them in conversation.
COPPERNOB.   What do I say ?
GINGERNUT.   Smile nicely at them and say, " Good morning, little ones, have you lost your way ? " and then you can offer to show them the way home.   Then make them sit down and rest, and then talk some more——
COPPERNOB.   What do I say then ?
GINGERNUT.   Tell them a story.   While you're telling them the story, I'll do the rest.
COPPERNOB.   Where will *you* be ?
GINGERNUT.   I'm going to hide over there (*points to bank back* o.).   All you've got to do is to make them watch *you* all the time.   Never mind about me.   Is that clear ?
COPPERNOB.   Yes, if *you* say so.
GINGERNUT (*annoyed*).   Don't keep on saying that ! (*He listens.*)   Quick, get ready !   I think I hear them coming.

(GINGERNUT *goes up to bank and passes behind it, showing his head over the top.*)

You do your stuff and I'll do mine.   (*Disappears behind bank.*)

(*The* BABES *enter from down* R., *hand-in-hand.*)

COPPERNOB (*imitating B.B.C. announcers*).   Hallo, twins !
BILLY.   Please, Mr. Man, we've lost our way.
COPPERNOB.   Lost your way, my little fledglings ? Well, now, isn't that careless of you ?

BETTY. Have *you* lost your way too ?

COPPERNOB. No, my little chickweed, Coppernob knows every path in this wood.

BILLY. Who's Coppernob ?

COPPERNOB. That's me.

BETTY. What a funny name !

(*The* BABES *giggle over this.*)

COPPERNOB (*aside*). They don't seem to be very frightened of me.

BILLY. Then you can show us the way home.

COPPERNOB. Of course I will, my little ducklings. But first of all, as this is the children's hour, you must sit down here and Uncle Coppernob will tell you a story.

(*The* BABES *sit down together, facing front,* COPPERNOB *on their* R.)

BETTY. Is it a good story ?

COPPERNOB. It's a wonderful story—(*aside*) if I can think of one.

BILLY. What's it about ?

COPPERNOB. It's about—it's about—(*aside*) what the devil is it about ?—(*To the* BABES.) It's about a—a bee-ootiful princess who—who used to walk every day in her garden—and—and dream of the good-lookin' prince she was going to marry, see ? (*Aside, mopping his brow.*) That's a good start.

BILLY. Did she walk in her sleep ?

COPPERNOB. No—she walked in her garden, I said.

BILLY. Then how could she have been dreaming ?

COPPERNOB (*getting annoyed*). Whose princess is she —yours or mine ? Don't interrupt the story. One day, as she was walking in her sleep—(*laughter from* BABES)—walking in her garden, I should say, two rob-bers decided to kidnap her and demand a ransom from the king.

BILLY. What's a ransom ?

COPPERNOB. A ransom is a sum of money—like what Uncle gives you every Saturday morning.

BETTY. Uncle never gives *us* any money. He's much too stingy.

COPPERNOB. That's because you ain't a princess.

(GINGERNUT *appears from behind the bank, with a sword in each hand, and begins to creep towards the* BABES, *looking murderous.*)

Well, the robbers appear suddenly from behind a bank and creep up behind the princess, and just as they are going to spring on her, a voice shouts out : " LOOK BEHIND YOU ! "

(COPPERNOB *shouts this out and the babes involuntarily look behind them. They see* GINGERNUT *with his swords raised to strike, shriek with fright and scramble off down* L. GINGERNUT, *enraged, bears down on* COPPERNOB.)

Oh, Gingernut, whatever *has* come over you ? You're looking quite bloodthirsty.

GINGERNUT. You've let them get away, that's why.

COPPERNOB (*sentimentally*). But surely you weren't going to kill those poor little children ?

GINGERNUT. Isn't that what we're here for ?

COPPERNOB. We're here to kidnap them, Ginger— not kill them. I've grown quite fond of those poor little mites.

GINGERNUT. What's that you say ? We'll see who's master here. I'll do this job myself, if you feel like that about it. But first of all, I'll put *you* out of the way, traitor. Will you fight ? (*Waves his sword about.*)

COPPERNOB. Yes, if *you* say so.

(COPPERNOB *draws his sword and* GINGERNUT *springs on him with a yell. Here follows a comic fight. The* VILLAINS *work their way up* R. *until* COPPERNOB, *who is being hard pressed, shouts out:* " Look behind you ! " *Off his guard,* GINGERNUT *looks the other way.* COPPERNOB *gives him a whack on the back of the head and runs off.* GINGERNUT *recovers himself and runs off* R. *in pursuit, leaving the stage empty. The* BABES *creep on from* L.)

BETTY. They've gone !

BILLY. What nasty men. They didn't seem to like each other much, did they ?

BETTY. Whatever shall we do now ?

BILLY. I think we'd better stay here. If we go on, we shall get loster and loster, shan't we ?

BETTY. I'm so tired. Let's sit down here and rest.

(The BABES lie down together on the bank. Incidental music and dim lights a little. After a pause the FAIRY trips on L., looks at the BABES and nods her head wisely.)

FAIRY. Yes, my little ones, I've been expecting you. Elves, come quickly !

(The ELVES run on from L. and R.)

You're going to be busy for once in your lives. Fetch leaves—big leaves—and cover up these poor mortals.

(The ELVES run off and return, each with a big leaf, which they place over the BABES until they are completely covered. A Ballet of Leaves can be suitably arranged here, if enough children are available.)

Now—if it rains, they won't get wet, and if it doesn't rain—well, they'll be dry, anyway. No one shall say that a fairy didn't know what to do in a situation like this.

(FAIRY trips up to the BABES, leans over them, waves her wand and speaks slowly through the music. Lights dimmer here.)

Sleep on, little mortals. No harm shall befall you under the magic canopy of leaves. Fairies are keeping watch and ward and you shall not wake until help comes from the friends who seek you.

(The lights fade out slowly and the CURTAIN is lowered to denote passage of time.)

SCENE 2.—*The same.   Lights up.*

(*The* FAIRY *and* ELVES *have disappeared but the* BABES *are still asleep under their leaves.   Bird warble as* CURTAIN *rises.   FRIAR TUCK is heard singing his song, off stage.   He enters* R., *singing.   The bird warble grows louder and disturbs him so that he stops singing and looks up to see where the bird is.*)

FRIAR.   There's some competition about.   (*Listens to the bird warble.*)   Shall it be said that I, Friar Tuck, was shouted down by a mere bird ?   Never !   (*To the orchestra.*)   Let's get on with the song.

(*He resumes his song number and the bird warble stops.*
At the end of his song he looks up again.)

I think I've silenced that bird this time.

(NURSE'S *voice is heard off* L., *sobbing.*)

Hullo !   There's another bird at it !   (*Listens.*)   Sounds like a corncrake.

(NURSE *enters, sobbing noisily.*)

My good woman, whatever *is* the matter ?
   NURSE (*between sobs*).   I—I'm n-not your g-good woman.
   FRIAR.   I wasn't talking in the—ahem—possessive sense.
   NURSE (*looking at him blankly*).   What *are* you talking about ?
   FRIAR.   I was endeavouring to enlighten myself as to the nature of your distress, my good—my good— *lady.*
   NURSE (*sobbing again*).   My poor babes !   They are lost !
   FRIAR   Ah, it is sad when a mother loses her babes.
   NURSE.   I—I'm not their mother——
   FRIAR (*raising his hands in astonishment*).   You are not the mother of your babes ?
   NURSE.   I'm their nurse, sir, but I love them as if they were my own

FRIAR (*sadly*). Ah! Never mind. They shall be found. I say so. (*Impressively.*) I am Friar Tuck, you know.

NURSE (*not impressed, and sobbing again*). I—I don't see that that makes any difference.

FRIAR. Have you never heard of the great Friar?

NURSE (*still not impressed*). No—what do you fry?

FRIAR (*aside*). The ignorance of these women! (*To* NURSE.) I will help you to find your babes.

NURSE (*gratefully falling into his arms*). Oh, Mr. Fryar!

FRIAR (*struggling to hold her up*). This is awkward!

(*Enter* ROBIN HOOD L., *followed by* ALLAN-A-DALE *and one or two of his men.* ROBIN *takes in the situation and laughs.*)

ROBIN. Look, Allan! Friar Tuck in the arms of a woman!

(FRIAR, *annoyed, pushes* NURSE *on to* ROBIN.)

FRIAR. Here, you take her! She's lost some children, or something. I was very foolish to have anything to do with her.

NURSE. My babes are lost in the forest, sir!

ROBIN (*comforting her*). We'll find them. Don't worry, my good woman.

FRIAR. I shouldn't call her that, if I were you. She doesn't like it.

NURSE (*looking at* ROBIN HOOD *rapturously*). I—I don't mind it—from you!

ROBIN (*winking at* FRIAR TUCK). *You've* got the bird!

FRIAR (*rudely*). If I may say so—*you* have the bird, and much good may she do you.

(FRIAR TUCK *exits* R. *in a huff.*)

ROBIN. Allan, take particulars.

(ALLAN *takes out a note-book and writes.*)

Let me have descriptions of your lost ones, madam, and
I will have the forest searched.

ALLAN (*writing*).   S.O.S.—Missing from their homes
—answering to the names of——

NURSE.   Betty and Billy.

ALLAN (*writing*).   Betty and Billy——

ROBIN.   Last seen at ?——

NURSE.   " The Four Feathers."

ALLAN (*writing*).   " The Four Feathers "——

ROBIN.   What were they wearing ?

(NURSE *describes the* BABES' *appearance, colour of hair,
    eyes, etc.,* ALLAN *taking down the particulars.   They
    are interrupted by a shout from one of the men who has
    been standing by the bank upstage.*)

MAN.   Master !   Are these what you are looking
for ?

(*The leaves on the bank move and the* BABES *are seen to be
    awake.   They sit up, yawn and stretch themselves.*
    NURSE *runs to them with cries of joy.*)

BILLY.   Hullo, Nurse !   Is it time to get up ?   (*Jumps
up.*)

NURSE.   My poor darlings, you must be perished with
cold and wet through !

BETTY (*springing up*).   I'm as warm as toast.   And
I've had such a lovely dream.

BILLY.   So have I.

(*The* BABES *come down* O., NURSE *between them.*)

ROBIN.   It looks as if they've been doped.   Have
they no father or mother ?

NURSE.   No, sir.   They are the nephew and niece
of the Baron and will have great wealth when they come
of age.

ROBIN.   The Baron !   Great wealth !   I smell foul
play !

ALLAN (*sniffing*).   I can't smell anything.

(ROBIN HOOD *takes* ALLAN *on one side.*)

Robin. Listen, Allan. I have a few old scores to pay off against the Baron. The babes may bring us luck. We will take them with us. (*To his men.*) Ho, there! Up with the little ones and let us continue our journey.

(*The men come forward and hoist the* Babes *on to their shoulders.*)

(*To* Allan.) We shall see—what we shall see.
  Allan (*mystified*). What shall we see?
  Robin (*mysteriously*). Wait and see!

(*The men form up, facing* R., *ready to take the road again.* Nurse *runs to* Robin Hood.)

Nurse. Will you please drop the babes at " The Four Feathers " ?
  Robin (*laughing*). We won't drop them. They're much too precious to drop. And we shall want *you* as evidence. Up with her too, men!

(*Two men hoist up the* Nurse, *who kicks and struggles.*)

Are we all ready? Forward to the Black Castle!

(*The orchestra plays a march as they file out.*)

Curtain.

ACT IV

The Hall of the Black Castle.

(*The principal entrance is through an arched doorway back
   c., to which three steps lead up from the stage.   Upper
   and lower side entrances.   A small throne on dais up
   R.*)

(*Festivities celebrating the re-opening of the Castle are in
   full swing.   SIR RICHARD'S guests are performing a set
   dance as the CURTAIN rises, after which SIR RICHARD
   appears at entrance back c.*)

SIR RICHARD.   Pray cease your revels one and all.
Ladies and gentlemen, we have an unexpected visitor.
(*Comes down c.*)   Prepare yourselves to do reverence to
His Majesty the King !

(*Two trumpeters appear back c. and blow a fanfare.   The
   KING enters between them, followed by the JESTER.   It
   is the JESTER's duty to blow a whistle which hangs round
   his neck every time the KING makes a joke, so that the
   people shall know when to laugh.   The guests have
   grouped R. and L and bow.   SIR RICHARD goes to the
   foot of the steps.*)

Welcome, your Majesty, to the Black Castle.

KING (*coming down steps to c., and gazing round at the
colours in the dresses and scenery*).   There's not much
" black " about it !

SIR RICHARD.   Your Majesty, on my return home
from the Crusades, I had the Castle done up throughout,
by (*local painter and decorator can be mentioned
here*).

KING.   Having " done you up," let's hope they
haven't " done you down."

(JESTER *blows his whistle. King looks round for laughter
but doesn't get any.*)

That didn't go very well.

SIR RICHARD. A thousand apologies, your Majesty.
Had your Majesty announced beforehand that you
intended to favour us with a joke, we would have been
prepared.

KING. Didn't you hear the whistle? When I make
a joke, my jester blows a whistle. It prevents people
laughing in the wrong place.

SIR RICHARD. Your Majesty is in a good humour
to-day.

KING. I am enjoying my tour through the provinces.
I had a fine day's hunting yesterday—killed three stags,
two bears and wounded the Sheriff of Nottingham.

SIR RICHARD. Not mortally, I hope, your Majesty.

KING. Only slightly. He got in the way of one of
my arrows, but didn't mind much. An arrow shot by
the King is nothing to make a(r)row about.

(JESTER *blows his whistle. There is some half-hearted
laughter by the guests. The KING looks disappointed.*)

The Sheriff told me you had returned from abroad, so
I thought, as I was passing, I would drop in and—er—
leave cards

(JESTER *takes from his tunic three large reproductions of
the playing-cards, KING, QUEEN and JACK, hands them
to SIR RICHARD and blows his whistle. Loud laughter
from everyone.*)

That's better. Now we all know each other.

(MARIAN *enters from down* L.)

SIR RICHARD. Your Majesty has yet to meet my
daughter.

(SIR RICHARD *presents MARIAN to the KING.*)

MARIAN (*kissing the KING's hand*). This is a great
pleasure for me, your Majesty.

KING (*eyeing her with great admiration*). It's not so bad for me, either. You may kiss our other hand.

(KING *extends his other hand, which is kissed by* MARIAN.)

A comely maid, Sir Richard. Our most valiant knight should not be ashamed to take her to wife.

SIR RICHARD. I fear maid Marian is rather head-strong, your Majesty.

MARIAN. I shall marry—when the right man comes along.

KING. And when the *right* man comes along, the others will be *left*.

(JESTER *blows his whistle. Laughter, in which the* KING *joins*.)

SIR RICHARD. Would your Majesty care to look over the Castle ?

KING (*surprised*). Look *over* it ? I'm not a giraffe.

SIR RICHARD (*embarrassed*). I mean—er, look—look *round* it, and partake of refreshment. I have some excellent wine——

KING. Lead the way ! And let the guests come too. I *may* want to make a few jokes on the way.

(SIR RICHARD, *the* KING *and* JESTER *move towards exit down* R. *The* BARON *emerges from the group of guests* R., *and kneels before the* KING.)

BARON. Your Majesty, I crave an audience.

KING. What is your business ?

BARON. I come in the interests of your loyal and faithful subjects to request you to grant an order for arrest.

KING. Arrest of whom ?

BARON. Robin Hood, the outlaw !

KING. I have heard of this Robin Hood. He is a harmless fellow enough.

BARON. He has robbed me of my children and holds them to ransom.

KING. Robin Hood a baby-snatcher ! This is a new line for him.

MARIAN. Your Majesty, there is some mistake. Robin Hood would not be guilty of such mean practices.

BARON (*angrily*). I tell you, the babes are in his keeping. He refuses to give them up.

KING. Tut! tut! Do not bandy words in the Royal presence. I will investigate this matter. It sounds interesting. In the meantime, Sir Richard, I think you mentioned refreshment—— (*He signs to* SIR RICHARD, *who shows the way off* R. *Music for the* KING'S *exit. The guests follow, leaving the* BARON *and* MARIAN *on the stage.*)

BARON (*advancing to* MARIAN, *who is down* L.). If you would screen Robin Hood, it will go ill with you. (*He shakes his fist in her face.*)

MARIAN. How dare you shake your fist at me, sir!

(BARON *turns away angrily and walks up* R., *turning at exit to deliver his parting threat.*)

BARON. I have knowledge that is dangerous to you. I have not forgotten that you took his gold!

(*Exits up* R.)

MARIAN. What a sinister old man. (*Comes* C.) I don't think I've seen the last of him. I suppose he's going to hide round corners and spy on me. I must try to look unconcerned. What does one do to look unconcerned? Hum a tune, or whistle? I can't whistle, unfortunately. I know! I'll sing and dance and that will show him I don't care a fig for his threats.

(MARIAN *gives a song number here, after which* ROBIN HOOD *appears back* C.)

ROBIN. I heard that. It was charming.

MARIAN (*down* L.). Robin! What are you doing here? You must go away at once.

ROBIN (*coming* C.). What! After all the trouble I've taken to get in? I expected at least to be asked to stay the week-end.

MARIAN. The King is here and the Baron seeks your life!

ROBIN (*laughing*).   Many men have wanted my life, Marian, but like most of us, they can't get what they want.

MARIAN.   Can't you get—what you want?

ROBIN.   I've come here to try.   (*Holds out his hand to her.*)

MARIAN (*drawing away from him*).   No, Robin, I—I shouldn't have said that.   You mustn't make love to me here.   Your life is in danger.   The King is not likely to treat you lightly.

ROBIN.   The King and I have never met, but—if we do, we shall get on very well, I've no doubt.   And as for the Baron—I have him on toast!

MARIAN.   He says you stole the babes.

ROBIN.   The babes are under my protection.   The old rascal tried to murder them in the forest.   I have the proof.

MARIAN.   I thought that old man was lying!   He had a shifty eye.

ROBIN.   He'll have a shifty neck too, when the rope's round it.   But we're wasting precious time, Marian.   I got you out of trouble once.   Will you do the same for me?

(MARIAN *goes to him* L.C., *anxiously*.)

MARIAN.   What is it, Robin?

ROBIN.   My trouble is that I—I want a wife.

MARIAN.   Is that a trouble?

ROBIN.   Yes—if she won't have me.

MARIAN (*faltering*).   I—I think she might——

(ROBIN *takes her in his arms in a long embrace.   The* KING *returns, unnoticed* R., *followed by* SIR RICHARD *and the* JESTER.   KING *stares at the couple, then clears his throat noisily.*   ROBIN HOOD *and* MARIAN *look up.*   MARIAN *gives a cry of alarm and runs away up* C.   ROBIN HOOD *holds his ground.*)

SIR RICHARD.   Robin Hood!

KING.   Ah!   So *this* is Robin Hood!

ROBIN (*bowing low*). Your Majesty's most humble and obedient servant.

KING. Humph! Neither humble nor obedient, if I am to believe the reports about you. Have you come to give yourself up?

ROBIN. Your Majesty, I have surrendered nothing but my heart.

KING (*looking at* MARIAN). I *thought* so. There's always a woman in the case.

SIR RICHARD. I had no idea of this!

KING. Of course you hadn't. Fathers are always the last to be told.

(SIR RICHARD *moves up to* MARIAN.)

Listen, Robin Hood. You are accused of baby-snatching,—an extraordinary crime for a man to commit who is—er (*looks at* MARIAN)—contemplating marriage.

ROBIN. I have two babes under my protection, sir——

KING. Where are they?

ROBIN. I have brought them with me. They await your Majesty's pleasure.

KING. Bring them here.

(ROBIN HOOD *bows and exits back* C.)

MARIAN (*kneeling to the* KING). Your Majesty, be merciful to Robin Hood. He is not capable of a mean action. If he holds the babes, it is surely for some just purpose.

KING. What say you, Sir Richard?

SIR RICHARD. I have found him a true man, sire. If you would be good enough to hear his case——

KING. Summon the guests, then. They shall be the Court. Order the Baron to wait on me immediately.

(MARIAN *exits* R.)

You haven't got a throne handy, I suppose?

SIR RICHARD (*leading the way to throne* R.). If your Majesty would deign to use this one——

KING (*seating himself uncomfortably*). It's pretty

hard ! That's the worst of these provincial thrones.
Next time I go on tour I shall bring my own.

(*Music.   The guests march in from back* C., *bowing to the*
KING *as they pass down stage,* R. *and* L.   *The* JESTER
stands above throne, SIR RICHARD *on* L. *of* KING,
MARIAN, *who has re-entered with guests, on* R.   *When
the stage is dressed,* ROBIN HOOD *and the* BABES *appear
back* C.   ROBIN HOOD *takes their hands and leads them*
C., *walking between them.   The* NURSE *follows behind.
The* BABES *are dressed in the green uniform of* ROBIN
HOOD'S *men.   The* NURSE *is dressed rather like a girl
guide, in green instead of blue.   The* BABES *each carry
a small bow, the arrows for which are seen protruding
from a small golf-bag which the* NURSE *carries slung
over her shoulder.*)

Hullo !—Twins !

(*General laughter from guests.   After laughter has sub-
sided,* JESTER *blows his whistle.*)

(*To* JESTER.)   Too late !   They've seen it already.

(*The* BABES *bow to the* KING.   *The* NURSE *bows so low
that all the arrows fall out of her bag.   Comic business
here.*)

ROBIN.   Your Majesty, these are the babes.
BILLY.   I'm not a babe now.   (*Proudly.*)   I'm one of
Robin Hood's merry men.   (*Aims his bow at the* KING
and is reproved by NURSE.)
ROBIN.   They have been fed and clothed by me, sire,
until such time as their case should be heard.
KING (*to* SIR RICHARD).   Summon the Baron to
attend the Court.

(SIR RICHARD *exits back* C.)

Robin Hood, how came these babes into your possession ?
ROBIN.   They were found by my men, abandoned in
the forest.
KING (*pointing to* NURSE).   And is she also an " abandoned " woman ?

NURSE. Me an abandoned woman ? I'm a respect-
able nurse, sir, and did my dooty in searching for them
until I had blisters on my feet—the poor little dears.

ROBIN. Had we not found them when we did, they
would undoubtedly have died of cold and hunger.
Suspecting foul play, I took them under my protection.

(SIR RICHARD *appears back o. and announces.*)

SIR RICHARD. The Baron !

(*The* BARON *enters back o., comes* R.O. *and bows to* KING.
SIR RICHARD *moves to* L. *of throne.*)

KING. Baron, are you the father of these rabbits ?

(*The* BARON *turns, sees the* BABES *and gives a start of
recognition. He shakes his fist at* ROBIN HOOD.)

Don't turn your back on the King. It isn't done !

BARON (*turning to* KING). I am the uncle of these
babes, sire. They were left under my care until they
come of age. But this scoundrel kidnapped them,
hoping to profit by such base procedure.

KING. Well, nunky, there they are. Kiss them and
make a fuss of them.

(BARON *approaches the* BABES, *who run away* L. *in a
fright. They are stopped by the* NURSE, *and hide
behind her.*)

They don't seem so pleased to see Nunky, after all.

ROBIN. Your Majesty, I can give a reason for that.
This man, this baron, sought their death. I accuse him
of attempting to murder these innocent children.

(*The guests register surprise.*)

KING (*rising*). What's this ? Murder ? Have you
the proofs ?

ROBIN. The proofs are here. (*Takes out a whistle
and blows it.*)

KING. Is this another joke ?

(*The two* VILLAINS *enter back* o.. *escorted by* LITTLEJOHN *and* ALLAN-A-DALE. *They come* C. BARON *moves down* R. ROBIN HOOD, *the* BABES *and* NURSE *are down* L.)

ROBIN (*stepping forward*). These two men, your Majesty, were employed by the Baron. They took his gold, in return for which they were to murder the babes in the wood. They confessed this to me, on pain of death.

(*The* VILLAINS *fall on their knees, trembling.*)

GINGERNUT. Your Majesty, we ask for pardon. We were tempted by the Baron's gold, but in the end, being good men and true, we could not do the deed.

KING (*to* COPPERNOB). Is this the truth ?

COPPERNOB (*almost too frightened to speak*). Y-yes— if y-you s-say so.

(GINGERNUT *gives him a disgusted look.*)

KING. I shall take no one's word. Let the babes decide as to who shall be their future protector.

BILLY
BETTY } (*together*). We choose Robin Hood !

KING. Out of the mouths of babes cometh forth wisdom.

(*The two* VILLAINS *withdraw upstage, with* LITTLEJOHN *and* ALLAN-A-DALE.)

BARON (*in a rage*). Is this justice ?

KING. No—it's common sense. (*Rises.*)

(BARON *registers defeat.* ROBIN *and the* BABES *come* C.)

ROBIN. I appreciate the honour conferred on me, but—(*looks at* MARIAN)—the babes will need a woman's care and affection. Sir Richard, I ask for your daughter's hand in marriage.

KING. I *thought* this was coming.

SIR RICHARD. Do you sanction this marriage, your Majesty ?

KING. I graciously do.

(MARIAN *runs to* ROBIN HOOD. *They embrace.*)

NURSE. But what about me ? I'm the nurse. Where do *I* come in ?

ROBIN (*smiling over his shoulder at her*). *You* come in through the servants' entrance.

NURSE (*bowing and in a servile tone*). *Very* good, sir.

KING (*who has come down* C. *with* JESTER). Oh, *very* good ! That's the best joke so far—(*regretfully*)—and I didn't make it—(*sharply to* JESTER, *digging him in the ribs*)—and *you* didn't see it ! (*He takes the* JESTER's *whistle and blows it himself. The guests laugh obediently and all principals should now be formed up downstage for the*

GRAND FINALE).

MADE AND PRINTED IN GREAT BRITAIN BY
LATIMER TREND & COMPANY LTD PLYMOUTH

www.ingramcontent.com/pod-product-compliance
Ingram Content Group UK Ltd.
Pitfield, Milton Keynes, MK11 3LW, UK
UKHW021822150726
72141PUK00017B/262